Original title:
Life's Meaning: A Joke with No Punchline

Copyright © 2025 Creative Arts Management OÜ
All rights reserved.

Author: Alec Davenport
ISBN HARDBACK: 978-1-80566-229-7
ISBN PAPERBACK: 978-1-80566-524-3

## The Comedian's Dilemma

In the spotlight, the punchlines fly,
Yet here I stand, my thoughts awry.
Laughter echoes, but where's the joke?
A twist in the tale, and it's all bespoke.

The crowd awaits with eager glee,
While I ponder deep, just let it be.
With a grin that's wide, yet no one sees,
The comic heart tucked in mysteries.

## A Playful Quandary

Tickle my toes with tales of the jest,
In this game of humor, I feel so blessed.
What makes them laugh? Is it truth or lies?
Or just the glitter in these jester's eyes?

A riddle of smiles, a whimsical spree,
Yet I sit pondering, oh woe is me!
Punchlines are dancing just out of reach,
In the quirks of this life, a lesson to teach.

## Echoes of Mirth

Giggling shadows play on the wall,
Whispers of laughter, they beckon and call.
What is it here that sparks the delight?
A chuckle, a snicker, a soft moonlit night.

In a world of jests where meanings entwine,
The punchline's a maze, nearly divine.
With each playful jab, I twist and I bend,
Searching for answers that seem never-ends.

## The Mimicry of Meaning

Mirror, mirror on the floor,
Tell me a joke, I implore!
Yet in this banter, the truth eludes,
A satire of life wrapped in good moods.

Punchlines are phantoms, they dance in my head,
While I chase shadows of words left unsaid.
With clownish attire and heart on my sleeve,
I jest and I jibe, do you dare to believe?

## A Comedy Without a Clue

In a room where laughter reigns,
Clowns shake hands with their own strains.
Jokes tumble, but none land right,
We giggle at the fading light.

Banana peels on polished floors,
With every trip, the slapstick soars.
Missteps dance with glee and cheer,
As we chuckle from ear to ear.

## The Irony of Unsaid Words

A wink exchanged, yet silence speaks,
The pun that's lost among the freaks.
A smile hides what hearts won't share,
The humor lingers in the air.

Whispers wrapped in foamy brews,
Words balloon yet never choose.
We laugh at what we never say,
In quiet corners, jokes decay.

## Jests Lost in the Abyss

In shadows where the humor hides,
A jest floats in the yawning tides.
Tickles echo in empty halls,
As punchlines play their silent falls.

A riddle weaves between the lines,
With answers lost, it never shines.
Grinning ghosts in timeless play,
As laughter fades, we drift away.

## The Whimsy of Fleeting Moments

Silly hats upon our heads,
Jokes exchanged like soft-spun threads.
A fleeting giggle, quick to part,
Yet lingers warmly in the heart.

Moments dance like butterflies,
On silly wings, our spirits rise.
In every chuckle, clouds drift by,
As fleeting whims begin to fly.

## **Serendipity in Silence**

In quiet corners laughter hides,
Where whispers giggle, softly glides.
The absurdity dances in the dark,
With shadows showing humor's spark.

A banana peel, a cosmic twist,
In stillness, mirth you can't resist.
Each chuckle more than just a sound,
In silent echoes, joy is found.

## **The Clown at Midnight**

A jester tiptoes through the night,
His painted grin, a comical sight.
With every stumble, joy appears,
As moonlight dances with our fears.

He juggles dreams and silly schemes,
In laughter's glow, we find our beams.
Each honk and wiggle brings delight,
As shadows twirl in pure moonlight.

## Shadows of a Forgotten Giggle

In corners where the giggles fade,
A shadow struts, unafraid.
It trips on memories, oh so bright,
And cracks the silence of the night.

Forgotten tales of whimsy past,
Each whispering chuckle, a spell cast.
From sorrow's grip, we soon escape,
With jesters' fables, laughter takes shape.

## Humor in Hues of Gray

In shades of gray, a riddle plays,
With punchlines lost in endless haze.
Yet joy emerges with a poke,
In grayest moments, laughter's cloak.

A wink, a smirk, a silly jest,
In simple things, we find our rest.
Though colors fade, our spirits rise,
In grinning shadows, laughter lies.

## Chuckles Between Stars

In the night sky, stars do wink,
They whisper secrets, laugh and think.
A comet zooms, a jester's flight,
While planets dance in pure delight.

Meteor showers, a giggling spree,
Tickling the cosmos, wild and free.
Galaxies spin, sharing their jest,
As universe plays, never a rest.

Asteroids tumble, tripping around,
With cosmic punchlines that know no bound.
Black holes play hide and seek so sly,
Swallowing humor as we all sigh.

So when you stargaze, make a wish,
For laughter's magic, a cosmic dish.
Among the twinkling, find your cheer,
For every giggle, a world is near.

## The Flicker of Humor

A candle flickers, shadows cast,
Whispers of laughter that surface fast.
With every glow, a tale is spun,
Of silly moments and endless fun.

The table's set for a joke or two,
Bantering friends, a lively crew.
They swap their stories, giggles collide,
In the glow of that candle, good vibes reside.

A spoonful of sugar, the old wise tale,
Turns frowning faces to gleeful inhale.
Laughter bubbles, like boiling tea,
In every cup, pure glee sets free.

So let the candlelight guide your night,
With chuckles to savor, the world feels bright.
In the flickering glow, find joy anew,
For humor's the glue that binds us true.

## Jokes That Drift Away

Floating on clouds, humor takes flight,
With silly thoughts that dance in the light.
A joke slips by, a feather soft,
Drifting far, that's how they loft.

Whispers of laughter ride on the breeze,
Tales that tickle and aim to please.
They paint the sky with colors bright,
While giggles echo through day and night.

A parrot squawks, "What's a funny bone?"
Answers escape, like an airy tone.
But the punchline flitters, lost in the air,
As we gather smiles, without a care.

So let the jokes drift, like wispy dreams,
In the fabric of laughter, find your beams.
For every chuckle that fancies to play,
Is a moment captured, never to sway.

## The Laugh That Lingers

In a bustling room, laughter ignites,
Spreading like wildfire, igniting the nights.
A tickle of whimsy, a jest that clings,
Making hearts dance as humor sings.

Punchlines miss, yet smiles bloom wide,
With bumbling stories we can't quite hide.
The echo of joy, it won't disappear,
Like bubbles in champagne, it's crystal clear.

Foolish antics, a game that we share,
With every giggle, burdens laid bare.
Life's little quirks, like a treasure chest,
In each laughter, we find our best.

So chase the chuckles, let them remain,
For in every giggle lies sweet refrain.
A gentle reminder, perhaps divine,
That joy's the connection, an endless line.

## Absurdities of Being

In a world of frolic and cheer,
We chase after dreams that disappear.
Each giggle wrapped up in a sigh,
What's the point? We just wave bye-bye.

The cat wears socks, a hat on its head,
While ducks recite what the toaster said.
Laughter spills like spilled milk on the floor,
We laugh till we can't, then we laugh more.

Why do we trip over our own two feet?
Chasing shadows, oh what a treat!
A jester's grin is a riddle unsolved,
In this play, we are all involved.

But what if the punchline took a day off?
Would we still giggle or just scoff?
So dance like no one is watching near,
And toast to the chaos, let's share a beer!

## Laughter in the Void

A wink from the stars, a chuckle from Mars,
We float in a universe painted with cars.
Why did the chicken cross the street?
To escape the punchline, can't take the heat!

Galaxies spinning like tops in a game,
Each twirl a riddle, none the same.
Tickle the cosmos, let out a snort,
In the absence of meaning, we're far from short.

Knocking on doors that don't even exist,
Searching for answers that curl like a fist.
The void chuckles back, oh what a tease,
It's all just a jape, the universe' ease.

So here's to laughter, the bubbles of air,
To juggling nonsense, we can all share.
In this cosmic dance, let's spin until dawn,
For meaning is hidden where laughter's drawn.

## Whispers of the Unseen

Dreams float by like whispers untold,
Wrapped in laughter, decorated in gold.
A banana peel waits to test your grace,
As we stumble through this bewildering race.

The moon plays tricks, gives the sun a nudge,
While we search for answers, we never budge.
Echoes of giggles fill empty rooms,
As we ponder in silence, while nothing looms.

Frogs talk philosophy without a cue,
Sipping on rain while they ponder the blue.
What's the punchline, oh where has it gone?
As we giggle, it's just us at dawn.

In this circus of quirks where we twirl,
Each misstep a dance, a cosmic swirl.
Let's embrace the absurd, as we chuckle along,
Together we moan, yet laugh in this song!

## Punchless Puzzles

A riddle wrapped in rubber bands,
Dancing about with jester hands.
Why does the clock tick without a sound?
Because it knows it's the punchline we found.

Each turn of phrase, a dizzying game,
With riddles that tease, and puzzles that flame.
We chase the punchline like a kid on a ride,
Only to find it's just gone to hide.

The fish in the sea wear tiny bow ties,
While apple trees break into surprise.
We tickle the funny till it runs away,
And in its absence, we still want to play.

So let's raise a toast to the riddles without,
To the laughs in the silence, the giggles about.
For in every jape, we find a strange thrill,
Punchless or not, we're dancing still!

## Mirth Without Reflection

A clown in a suit, what wisdom he'd share,
With rubbery shoes and a colorful hair.
He juggles our worries, a pie in the face,
Yet still we wonder, is this all a race?

The sun shines so bright, but he trips on a stair,
His laugh fills the room, yet it's caught in mid-air.
With smiles lighting paths, like fireflies in flight,
We giggle and stumble, through day into night.

## The Unspoken Jest

Two chairs holding secrets, they whisper and tease,
One leans to the left, the other, at ease.
A wink and a nod, but what's really the joke?
Maybe it's weather, or perhaps just a poke?

A cat in a hat, he struts down the lane,
He trips over socks, now that's truly insane!
Yet laughter escapes, like bubbles in air,
While pondering deeply, is anyone there?

## A Sunset of Silliness


The moon wears a grin, with stars as his friends,
While laughter erupts, as the daytime light ends.
The sun gives a bow, in a flare of bright hues,
While crickets recite their own rhythmic snooze.

A bubblegum pop, and a twirl on the grass,
As fireflies dance, oh, what a fine class!
They all share a secret, without cluing us in,
Oh, the punchline is missing, let the show begin!

**The Curiosity of Chuckles**

In a land where the jesters sprout like the trees,
Giggling squirrels conspire, substituting keys.
A banana peel's lurking, it waits with a grin,
As we chase our own tails, let the laughter begin.

A knock at the door, it creaks and it wobbles,
Are we expecting jokes, or just mischievous gobbles?
Mirth's tangled in riddles, we ponder and sway,
While the world winks at us, in its silly ballet.

## **Laughter on a Lonely Path**

Once I tripped on my own feet,
And laughed till I cried, can't be discreet.
The sun shone bright, but oh what a tease,
As I danced with shadows, trying to please.

A squirrel mocked me, held its chest,
It seemed to say, 'You're quite the jest!'
With every hiccup, I sang a tune,
In a world absurd, gone mad by noon.

**The Quirk of Existence**

A kangaroo hops in a business suit,
With a tie that flaps, how absolute!
He checks his watch, it's time for lunch,
But there's only grass, oh what a crunch!

Two pigeons gossip on a park bench,
About the news that makes no sense.
"Why did the chicken cross the way?"
"Just for a laugh at the end of the day!"

## The Apathy of Humor

I told a joke to a silent tree,
It stood there, not a chuckle was free.
The wind just sighed, a leaf took flight,
Guess it didn't find my humor quite right.

A crow cawed loud, mocking my plight,
Was it a jest or just sheer spite?
With every pun, my spirit sank,
Yet in the dark, I drew a prank.

## The Ripple of a Quiet Joke

In a corner cafe, a grin so sly,
A waiter slipped, let out a cry.
Coffee so hot, the cups all danced,
While patrons chuckled, all entranced.

A cat in a window, sage and wise,
Half-asleep, watching diners' fries.
With eyes that twinkled like bright stars,
It pondered deeply, the meaning of spar.

## Whispers of Joy Around Empty Tables

In the corner laughs a shadow,
A joke that's lost its way,
Chairs that creak with stories,
But no one's here to stay.

The candle flickers, dim and bright,
Flicking off unseen tears.
A punchline waits in silence,
Echoing through the years.

The wine glass jokes with no one,
As crumbs debate in a heap,
A banquet of wishes scattered,
But laughter's in deep sleep.

Tables dressed in memories,
With ghosts of cheer around,
Here's to the banter never shared,
Where joy's just barely found.

## The Giggle Stuck in My Throat

I swallowed a laugh this morning,
Like a gumball stuck tight,
It dances on my tongue still,
Wishing for the light.

Every pun's a little monster,
That tickles me inside,
But when I try to share it,
My chuckles start to hide.

Conversations full of laughter,
But the punchline's all alone,
Giggling in my belly,
Like an unsung, sad trombone.

It's a joke without an ending,
A riddle with no clue,
And yet it keeps on bubbling,
Like laughter's overdue.

## Smiles That Hide a Deeper Truth

Behind the grin there's chaos,
The humor's just a mask,
For every quirky giggle,
Hides questions none would ask.

In each bright-eyed expression,
A secret waits to burst,
Like rainbows in a thunderstorm,
The giggles thrust and cursed.

They smile like painted daisies,
But roots fester deep within,
Unraveling the joy we flaunt,
As if it's all a sin.

So let's poke at the laughter,
And see what's underneath,
For smiles may tell a story,
Of mischief and of grief.

## **Playfulness Between the Lines**

In scribbles and strange doodles,
Lies humor tucked away,
A joke that could be funny,
If I could just convey.

Every lyric brings a chuckle,
Yet meanings twist and dip,
I laugh amidst the confusion,
As words take a sly trip.

Between the cracks of giggles,
Lies wisdom soft and sly,
A punchline that's elusive,
A wink with a wise eye.

So here's to all the funny,
In riddles we disguise,
Where playfulness ignites the heart,
And joy wears funny ties.

## Where Wit Meets the Infinite

A clown walks a tightrope, high and thin,
His feet tap dance while the world spins.
Gravity giggles, takes a nap,
As laughter drips from my funny cap.

Upon the moon, a cat plays chess,
While wise old owls share their stress.
The stars chuckle, forming their jokes,
As planets wobble in comedic pokes.

Brass bands play in the void so grand,
While silly things don't go as planned.
A rubber chicken drops with a plop,
And echoes ring until they stop.

The punchline comes as a gentle sigh,
From cosmic jesters who pass by.
With every twist and silly quirk,
The universe laughs, it just won't work.

## Amusement in the Face of Mystery

In shadows, a riddle wears a grin,
Jesters propose the wildest spin.
A turtle races, a snail laughs loud,
While clouds wear hats, looking proud.

The moonlight snickers, casting its beam,
Illuminating chaos, a shared dream.
Balloons drift high on thoughts of cheer,
As the night whispers, 'Worry not, dear!'

A magician's cat ponders its tricks,
While rabbits hop in a dance of flicks.
Mysteries settle in a playful game,
And questions arise that stay the same.

Yet amid this fun, the truth slips free,
Wrapped in laughter, it calls to me.
With every giggle, we come to find,
The answers hide, forever unlined.

## The Jest That Time Forgot

Tick-tock went the clock in a jive,
While seconds chuckled and tried to thrive.
Time wore a hat, oversized and bright,
As moments danced into the night.

A butterfly whispered a sailor's tale,
Of fish in the sky and an empty sail.
As years flew by on a unicycle,
The horizon laughed in a playful cycle.

Every memory spun like a top,
The icicles grinned, ready to drop.
With jokes unspoken, time held its breath,
As humor evolved, evading death.

The jest hangs loose like a pantsless king,
In a court of giggles, where dreams take wing.
Though time may fade, the laughter will stay,
An echo of joy in a wondrous play.

## Puns from the Depths of Despair

In shadows deep, where rueful sighs,
The grinning clowns wear puzzled eyes.
A broken record spins a tune,
As laughter creeps in, a cheeky boon.

A darkened room with a single light,
The jokes collide in a playful fight.
The punchline hides, a sneaky sprite,
In corners where shadows dare to bite.

From depths of gloom, a pun takes flight,
As uproarious laughter conquers night.
The more we frown, the funnier grows,
Like onions in stories, layer by rows.

So even when despair paints worlds in gray,
Let humor persist in a fanciful way.
Amidst the woes, a chuckle will bloom,
Turning heavy hearts into humor-filled rooms.

## Mirth in the Midst of Mayhem

In chaos we dance, with glee in our eyes,
The jester's call echoes, under stormy skies.
A banana peel slips, oh what a sight,
Laughter erupts, in the dead of the night.

With each silly fall, we gather round tight,
The punchlines escape, like a kite in full flight.
Carrots in hats, and socks with no shoes,
We giggle at life, with colorful hues.

## The Silence of Gags

A mime tries to speak, but no words come through,
His gestures so grand, yet we haven't a clue.
Invisible walls, and ropes that he tugs,
We laugh till we cry, at his comical shrugs.

In awkward silence, jests take their flight,
A wink, and a grin, make the dullness feel bright.
In the stillness we find the humor we seek,
For laughter's pure charm can be wonderfully meek.

## Puns Beneath the Surface

Beneath all the surface, a pun starts to brew,
Like fish at a party, they wiggle and skew.
With each clever quip, the laughter takes flight,
Leaving us chuckling well into the night.

A tomato walks into a bar, feeling spry,
With a joke in its pocket, it leaves by and by.
Onions give layers; they cry in delight,
As humor unfolds, banishing fright.

## Absurd Reflections

In mirrors we see all the odd little quirks,
A dancing sock puppet, how it truly lurks.
Reflections that giggle and titter with glee,
As shadows perform in a wild jamboree.

A clock with no hands just won't take the bait,
It ticks and it tocks, but it's always too late.
With irony hanging like fruit on a vine,
We toast to the strange, our glasses align.

## The Last Laugh Unheard

In the corner, a chuckle lingers,
Yet the punchline's lost in air.
The audience, they point and ponder,
What was funny? Did we care?

A comedian slips on a banana,
But the peel is where joy resides.
We laugh at things so mundane,
And then question why laughter hides.

The clown juggles with perfect practice,
Yet his heart's heavy with dread.
We clap and cheer for the laughter,
As silence hangs, filled with lead.

So here's to jokes that wander,
With no reason left to explain.
We share a grin, then grow ponder,
The joke was funny, yet so plain.

## Jests That Fade Away

A whisper flies like feathers,
On the breeze of absent cheer.
We chuckle at silly blunders,
But fade, when no one's near.

Like shadows on the sidewalk,
Those quips they flit and flee.
The more we try to catch them,
The less they seem to be.

A riddle wrapped in laughter,
Left unanswered on the floor.
We seek a hearty answer,
But find ourselves back for more.

Every giggle hides a secret,
That swiftly drifts to night.
We enjoy the jest of jesting,
Yet miss the final sight.

## **Banter Beneath the Surface**

With a wink and a nudge we gather,
Around the tales both tall and small.
Yet under the banter's laughter,
A silence looms, quiet for all.

The jokes they swirl like confetti,
Unraveled in our minds so bright.
Yet hidden beneath the chuckles,
Are truths lost in the night.

We poke fun at the dullest matters,
Spin yarns that dance on air.
But when the laughter fades to whispers,
What's left? Just a vacant stare.

So here's to jesters of all ages,
Who shine but never really know.
The laughter spins into stages,
Yet the meaning drifts and flows.

## The Paradox of Grins

A smile breaks while shadows cover,
Beneath the joy, a waiting jest.
We beam, while frowning skips the hover,
Revealing gags that offer rest.

A child laughs at a simple falling,
While grown-ups roll their eyes in tease.
Yet wisdom hides in humor's calling,
Beneath the surface, truths can freeze.

Tickles tickle, yet questions linger,
Why's the punchline not profound?
We jest, while fate upholds its finger,
Lost laughs reverberate around.

So cheers to those who laugh unknowing,
With joy that leaves us slightly stuck.
For in the jest, a truth is showing,
We find our fun—yet—what the luck?

# The Enigma of Existence

In the circus of thoughts, we all play our part,
Clowns of confusion, with a wink and a start.
Juggling the questions, we toss in the air,
Giggling madly at the weight of despair.

Smiles can be masks, or they might be the truth,
A riddle wrapped up in a candy-coated sleuth.
We chase after answers, like cats on the chase,
While shadows of wisdom dance in empty space.

With laughter as syrup, we drown every fear,
Yet the punchline eludes us, it's nowhere near.
We scribble the script, but the pages run dry,
As the punchline gets lost like a balloon in the sky.

So we chuckle and wonder, in this grand charade,
As the punchline awaits in the jester's parade.
The mystery lingers, with giggles and glee,
A cosmic inside joke, just you and me.

## An Infinite Jest

Bubbles of laughter float high in the air,
Words tumbling down with a comedic flair.
We stand on the stage, the spotlight is bright,
But the joke's on us in the dark of the night.

The audience chuckles, their faces aglow,
As we spin around tales that have nowhere to go.
With timing impeccable, though awkward the tune,
We salute the absurd 'neath the smirk of a moon.

Tickling the fancies, we prance and we trot,
As the punchline teases, but it's still not what's sought.
We laugh in the chaos, we dance in the haze,
Unsure if it's funny or just a strange phase.

Yet still, we persist, with our hearts in our hands,
Crafting the humor that life never plans.
For deep in the punchline, if ever it's found,
Is the joy of the journey, the laughter unbound.

## Laughing in the Dark

In the shadows we gather, with giggles and sighs,
Trading our dreams for some whimsical lies.
Though the night seems so quiet, it's ripe with delight,
As we stumble on humor hidden from sight.

We wear our best masks, with grins painted bright,
But the punchline's elusive, just out of our sight.
We trip on the echoes of laughter that rings,
In the corners of minds where the silly heart sings.

Chasing the tail of a cat that won't stay,
We ponder the stories of night and of day.
With each twist and turn, we discover the jest,
A riddle unraveled, a flutter, a quest.

So we laugh in the dark, like stars in a blur,
With joy that's contagious, unsure of the spur.
For the heart knows the punchline, though not in plain sight,
As we dance with the shadows, and bask in the light.

## The Unfinished Punchline

In a world full of quips, the jesters abound,
With humor that teeters and spins round and round.
We gather in circles, exchanging our yarns,
But the end of the story is lost in the dawns.

We craft clever tales, with wit as our glue,
Yet somehow the laughter feels soured and blue.
The punchline eludes us like shadows that flee,
As we question the jest in all that we see.

With echoes of laughter that dance on the breeze,
We barter our smiles, hoping they bring us ease.
But the joke seems unfinished, a riddle thus thrown,
Leaving us giggling, yet never alone.

So we chuckle and ponder, adrift in our mirth,
For the punchline's a treasure, untouched since our birth.
Yet in every good chuckle lies wisdom's embrace,
A reminder to savor each fleeting trace.

## Whims of the Wandering Heart

A cat in a hat sings a tune,
While cows dance around a full moon.
Socks lost in the wash, they giggle aloud,
As toast takes a leap, brave and proud.

A frog wears glasses, reading a book,
In a park where the squirrels all cook.
Life's little quirks keep us amused,
With each twist and turn, we're gently bruised.

Birds crack jokes on a high, swaying wire,
While shoes tap away to rhythm and fire.
A world so silly, absurd yet fun,
Where the punchlines hide, but the laughter's begun.

## Jest By Candlelight

In shadows that twirl like a dancer's delight,
A spoon tells a story by candlelight.
With forks as the audience, they laugh and gleam,
As shadows weave tales from a whimsical dream.

A ghost in a top hat shimmies with flair,
While mice in bow ties debonair.
The clock ticks in rhythm, no time left for fate,
For laughter's the answer, we patiently wait.

Chairs crack a joke, benches join in,
Each wall whispers secrets, a grand little din.
The punchlines are missing but fun flows in streams,
As we gather round, cradled in dreams.

## The Grin That Outlasted Time

A clock on the wall wears a whimsical face,
Ticking in rhythm, it quickens the pace.
With a wink and a smile, it dances around,
While socks swapped their places, now lost, never found.

A parrot in pajamas repeats all the jest,
As time chews its gum, taking life as a test.
Frogs in high heels twirl on a stage,
With laughter so contagious, it steals every page.

The world spins a yarn, not bothered by rhyme,
For the grin on our faces could outlast the time.
With quirks and oddities shaping our fate,
We chuckle and shake, happily late.

## Absurdity Adrift

A bicycle swims in the ocean so blue,
While fish throw confetti, those jesters in queue.
The sun wears a hat, tipping it low,
As clouds whisper secrets from high, soft and slow.

A banana slips gracefully on its peel,
As clouds are in stitches, unable to heal.
Chairs dance in circles, and cats sing a tune,
In a world of silly where whimsy's our boon.

Through tangled vines and odd, tangled dreams,
Absurdity floats on like candy bar streams.
With laughter as currency, life's quirks teach,
That there's more to behold than the punchline we reach.

## **The Echo of a Forgotten Chuckle**

In a room full of grins, there's a laugh that won't fade,
The punchline is lost, yet we've all been played.
A wink in the corner, a nod from the cat,
We ponder the humor in a lost wooly hat.

The clown in the mirror just painted his nose,
But nobody's laughing, as everybody knows.
The pie on the floor, a slip and a slide,
Yet still we are dancing with folly our guide.

A tickle in the air, but it's paper mache,
We're rolling in giggles and lost in dismay.
The joke's on the clock, it's a pun in disguise,
With laughter still echoing, truth underlies.

Between every chuckle, a silence lurks near,
We throw out a riddle while sipping our beer.
An enigma that tickles both mind and the gut,
A joke with no end, forever a rut.

## Jests Amidst the Chaos

A cat wearing glasses is chasing its tail,
The dog might just join in this whimsical trail.
A fish starts to dance, while the frog plays the flute,
Together they form quite the raucous salute.

The jester forgot where he put down his shoe,
The audience giggles, unsure what to do.
Every tumble and trip turns into a cheer,
Each stumble a moment we hold very dear.

Muffins are flying like comets in space,
Sugar on our faces, we laugh in this race.
But why are we baking when chaos is high?
Perhaps just for fun, or to see muffins fly.

A whisper of humor floats up to the sky,
While the toaster revolutionizes how we fry.
In the heart of the madness, a jest will appear,
Reminding us all why we gather right here.

# The Comedy of Errors

In a play that's forgotten, the actors all sigh,
The script was a riddle, but no one knows why.
A banana peel slips 'neath the curtain so sheer,
The audience chuckles, "Oh dear, oh dear!"

The clock strikes a laugh as the cat takes a bow,
While the dog steals the show, and we wonder just how.
Every mix-up is mirrored in bright spotlight beams,
Creating a world where we laugh at our dreams.

With every misstep, a chuckle will rise,
As the punchline eludes, spinning tales and ties.
A ticket to folly, that's what we all seek,
In the fluff of absurdity, smiles at its peak.

Upon the stage of mishaps, we dance with delight,
Painting the air with laughter, our spirits take flight.
As errors unfold like a whimsical play,
The charm of the jesters will never decay.

## The Smirk Without a Reason

On a street paved with giggles, a smirk starts to roam,
Searching for laughter, but far from a home.
With pockets of irony, filled till they're tight,
Each chuckle's a question, evading the light.

A sandwich in hand, it accidentally flies,
Landing in laughter, much to our surprise.
We gather around, as we munch and we share,
The humor of snacks scattered out in mid-air.

A penguin in slippers just walked down the lane,
With each little wobble, we burst out in gain.
The silliness thrives, and the odd just feels right,
In a world that's so curious, we cherish the night.

So here's to the smirk that has no reason why,
As we lift up our heads, let our spirits comply.
In the absence of answers, we giggle and spin,
Finding joy in the drift of a whimsical grin.

## Echoes of a Silent Punchline

A cat with shades, lounging in style,
Dreams of fish with a cheeky smile.
The clock ticks loud, but what's the time?
Who knew a joke could feel like a rhyme?

The chairs are laughing, they're losing their grip,
As we dance the tango on a banana slip.
A parrot reads jokes, but forgets the laughs,
While we gather the crumbs from the just-nibbled halves.

The light bulb flickers, is it out of gas?
Or perhaps it just knows this too shall pass.
Knock-knock on shadows, they hide and peek,
Whispering secrets that feel rather bleak.

Yet still we chuckle, as we fall into sleep,
Embracing the mysteries that make us weep.
In the end, we find, it was all just a jest,
The punchline evades, but we're still very blessed.

## The Paradox of Smiles and Shadows

A shadowy grin walks into the sun,
Says, 'Let's play hide-and-seek, it'll be fun!'
But no one replies, they're busy and deep,
In thoughts of the laughter that never will leap.

The moon offers jokes, they float on a breeze,
Tickling the stars, with whims like a tease.
A table of souls hum softly in glee,
Yet punchlines are played on their own, you'll see.

The road is a carpet of tripping delight,
As travelers wander, seeking the light.
But the closer they get, the more it eludes,
Painting the day in absurditudinal moods.

Grab the popcorn, for this show is the best,
With scenes of confusion that leave us all stressed.
And while we stand tall with our laughter in tow,
The punchlines just slip, like a whispered hello.

## Teetering on the Edge of Oblivion

On the edge of a giggle, we balance and sway,
Where nonsense and reason decide to play.
A dog in a bowtie, with elegance grand,
Reveals the punchlines, but leaves them unmanned.

We juggle our stories, like clowns at a fair,
With laughter like bubbles that fill up the air.
But just at the peak of our comedic delight,
A tumble, a stumble, we vanish from sight.

A light-hearted echo rings through the void,
As we ponder the punchlines we've personally foiled.
We serve up the jokes on a platter of fate,
Yet somehow, the setup is always too late.

Still, we keep tossing our thoughts in the air,
Like popcorn in butter, beyond all despair.
And so in the chaos, we find our own glee,
Teetering ever, on the edge of what could be.

## Humor in the Void

In a galaxy filled with invisible glee,
A comet delivers its best memory.
We chase after echoes in dark swirls of night,
Wondering, were we wrong or just losing our sight?

The universe chuckles, it spins without care,
As we toss our jokes into cosmic air.
Yet silence responds with a whisper so slight,
Leaving our punchlines out of the light.

As planets align with a rhythm divine,
We sit on the sidelines, drink coffee and whine.
A waiting room filled with deep-sighing woes,
Turns into a circus where humor still grows.

In the laughter of stardust, we'll find what we seek,
Even if punchlines decide to play hide and seek.
So toast to the absence of what we can't speak,
For in clouds of confusion, we're all kind of meek.

## The Parable of Forgotten Puns


In a world where laughter's lost,
Jokes are shared, but at what cost?
A punchline waits, but wanders far,
Leaving grins that barely spar.

The jester trips, his shoes untied,
With every slip, the crowd can't hide.
He tells a tale both dull and pale,
As punchlines drift like wind's soft wail.

A wink, a giggle, a silent cheer,
Why are we laughing? Oh, dear, oh, dear!
Life's a stage with no final act,
The funny bits are all abstract.

So gather round for one more jest,
In this riddle, we find our quest.
With puns forgotten, here we toil,
In giggly confusion, we share the spoil.

## Mirth in the Margins

In the corners, humor hides,
Between the lines, the laughter bides.
A misplaced quote, a twist of fate,
Brings smiles upon the heavy plate.

Notes scribbled wildly, a puzzled frown,
Turns frustration upside down.
Every chuckle, a hidden gem,
In the margins, the world's a whim.

Why fit in? Why take a bow?
When nonsense reigns, let humor plow.
The punchlines linger, just out of sight,
Like shadows dancing in the night.

So flip the page, adjust your lens,
Find joy where logic merely bends.
In laughter's echo, our spirits soar,
Each chuckle lingers, forevermore.

## Chasing the Elusive Chuckle

I chased a laugh through fields of green,
Where giggles play and joke's unseen.
A fleeting grin, a winking stare,
The chuckle hides behind thin air.

I asked a tree, where jesters dwell,
It rustled leaves, said, "Can't you tell?"
The best of jokes just twirls away,
Leaving us grinning in disarray.

In every corner, a whisper spins,
With puns that tease but never wins.
Like clouds that float on a sunny day,
Chasing humor is the game we play.

So if you stumble upon a tickle,
Don't let it go—just give a wiggle.
For laughter's echo can fade so fast,
The chuckle chased, but never grasped.

## The Smirk of the Universe

The cosmos chuckles in midnight hue,
With stars that snicker and wink at you.
A comet trails a cheeky jest,
While black holes swallow humor's quest.

Galaxies twist in playful flight,
Creating laughter from day to night.
With meteors that tease and gleam,
Life's a comic, or so it seems.

Quasars beam a poke at fate,
As planets dance, don't hesitate.
In cosmic puns and stellar fun,
We find the grins where we begun.

So leap among the giggling skies,
Open your heart to the universe's sighs.
In every twinkle lies a joke,
Forever smirking, as worlds evoke.

## Shadows of Laughter

In a world of quirks and twists,
We dance on dreams, a laugh persists.
The punchlines hide, they tease and play,
As shadows giggle, they fade away.

A jester's cap upon our heads,
We tread the path where humor threads.
With folly's grin, we twirl and spin,
In this grand farce, we all must win.

The sun pokes fun, the moon will jest,
Each tick of time, a quirky quest.
Through giggles bright and chuckles wide,
We ride the waves, a joyful tide.

So raise a glass to riddles grand,
To life's absurd, not quite what planned.
In every laugh, a truth we find,
With shadows dancing, hearts unconfined.

## Witty Whispers of the Cosmos

Stars twinkle with a wink so sly,
The universe laughs with a cosmic sigh.
Galaxies spin their tales untold,
In the tapestry, jokes unfold.

Planets guffaw in an endless jest,
As comets race, they're never stressed.
A black hole chuckles, pulling us near,
With infinite jokes, and no end here.

Astronauts giggle in zero-grav flight,
Chasing stardust through the night.
With witty whispers, the cosmos play,
Life's cosmic punchlines drift away.

So next time you gaze at the night,
Remember the laughter, the pure delight.
In every star and every wave,
Witty echoes, the brave and the grave.

## Jest in the Journey

On roads unknown, we laugh and roam,
With silly antics, we find our home.
In every turn, a jest awakes,
As we dance through life's great mistakes.

Traveling light with a wink and grin,
We wear our mishaps as our skin.
The map is scribbled, directions wrong,
Yet every detour leads to song.

With every stumble, a laugh we share,
Life's playful nudges, beyond compare.
A twist in fate, a ticklish bend,
In jest we find the joy we send.

So let's raise a toast to roads less paved,
To the goofy routes that we've all braved.
In every chuckle, a bonding thread,
In the journey, let laughter be wed.

## The Prank of Perpetuity

Time pulls pranks with a sly little smile,
Stretching minutes into a while.
We chase the clock, a comical race,
Yet find ourselves in a timeless space.

With every tick, a giggle escapes,
As seconds twist into funny shapes.
The past and future, a playful tease,
In the grand scheme, we laugh with ease.

Eternity's jest, a loop so tight,
Where moments collide, day meets night.
We learn to laugh at each grand design,
In the prank of time, all is divine.

So let's chuckle at what's yet to come,
As we join the dance, a cosmic drum.
In this endless journey, we're not alone,
For humor binds each heart and bone.

## The Absurdity of Everyday Whispers

In the morning, toast burns nice,
But the coffee can't pay the price.
The cat mimes a serious stare,
Yet sleeps without a single care.

Children giggle at silly jokes,
While dogs ponder on the folks.
A squirrel steals a bit of pie,
And wonders if he's meant to fly.

Lost socks plot their escape plans,
While dust bunnies form secret clans.
We laugh to mask the simple truth,
That absurdity holds the fountain of youth.

A banana peels in grand delight,
As it slips past the tree at night.
Who knew chaos wore a crown?
Yet here we are, forever clown.

## The Unfinished Riddle of Existence

What's the answer to the riddle?
A chicken stuck in a fiddle?
Questions dance like awkward feet,
While the answers take a seat.

Why do we break for lunch at noon?
Maybe to laugh at the moon.
Or ponder why socks never pair,
With oddities lurking everywhere.

The math of life does not add up,
Like sipping from a half-filled cup.
Yet every curveball brings a cheer,
As puns and giggles reappear.

A fortune cookie cracks a grin,
With wisdom lost, where to begin?
In every pause, there's room for fun,
Yet the riddle's never quite done.

## Laughing in the Shadow of Uncertainty

In shadows where the question creeps,
Laughter stirs and softly peeps.
Life's a circus, many rings,
Where certainty is not a thing.

We juggle dreams and silly fears,
With clowns that wipe away our tears.
Each twist and turn, a crazy ride,
Inside our hearts, we'll always hide.

If time is just a floppy shoe,
Then fork it out, go find the glue.
For in the dance of mixed-up fate,
A smile is sure to gravitate.

In shadowy corners, jokes grow tall,
While we hold hands and take the fall.
With each good laugh, we cease to care,
That here and now is all we share.

## When the Puns Fall Flat

Two peas in a pod, tight and snug,
Tumble out, then give a shrug.
They chuckle soft, then roll away,
At puns that flopped like yesterday.

A joke's a seed in muddy ground,
Where laughter sometimes can't be found.
Yet knock-knock jokes still knock about,
Oldies but goodies, there's no doubt.

The punchline lands with quite a thud,
But the setup loves to make a bud.
In every stumble, giggles spark,
A spark that shines within the dark.

So raise your glass to wit and jest,
And find the cracks that make it best.
For even when humor hits a snag,
The heart still dances, laughs can drag.

## The Invisible Punchline

In a world where laughter reigns,
We search for clues in silly plains.
A jester's hat without the jest,
A punchline lost, but we're still blessed.

Funny faces, rolling eyes,
Chasing giggles, dodging sighs.
Where's the humor, can you see?
Or is it hiding, just like me?

A banana peel, a slip, a fall,
We trip on jokes, we fear the call.
Silence echoes, waiting, craving,
For a punchline that keeps misbehaving.

The laughter hangs, a distant friend,
A tickle in the mind, no end.
So let's revel in this fuzzy state,
Where fun is good, and we wait on fate.

## **The Dance of the Unfathomable**


Two left feet on a dancing floor,
Twirl and stumble, ask for more.
The music plays, it's quite absurd,
We laugh together, without a word.

In circles spun, we drift, we sway,
Chasing shadows in the fray.
Do we know the steps, not at all,
Yet here we are, ready to fall!

A partner joins, a silly jig,
Defying logic, life's a gig.
The rhythm sways, the night's so bright,
Why search for reason, just hold on tight!

In foolish fate, we're all entwined,
With every glance, a laugh aligned.
So dance with me 'til dawn's first light,
In the absurdity, we'll find delight.

**Smiles in the Unknown**

There's a tickle in the cosmic void,
A chuckle shared, perhaps enjoyed.
Giggles echo in the dark,
Who knew absurd could leave a mark?

A rubber chicken in the sky,
With each new riddle, we ask why.
The stars align in silly ways,
As laughter fills our wandering days.

Guesswork wraps our fragile dreams,
In the silence, humor beams.
Do answers hide or slip away?
We laugh aloud, come what may!

So in the unknown, smiles we share,
An empty punchline filled with air.
In every giggle, find the cheer,
And in the riddle, gather near.

## **The Quip That Never Landed**

A punchline tossed like a paper plane,
It soars and twists, but brings no gain.
Falling flat with graceful flair,
Like awkward humor, trapped in air.

Knock-knock jokes, they come and go,
But wait—who's there? I just don't know!
Absurdity beckons, oh so bright,
Yet still the quip takes flight at night.

Wordplay dances on a thread,
With every giggle, mischief's spread.
Did we miss the point or find new ground?
In every laugh, a truth profound.

So here we stand, on stage alone,
Embrace the funny, claim your throne!
For in the mishap, joy we find,
The quip that didn't land, unconfined.

## The Parable of the Missing Punchline

In a world where laughter flies,
The punchline travels, but never arrives.
We tickle fates with giggles rare,
Yet lost in clouds, it hangs in air.

A jester frowns, his crown askew,
He tells a tale, but no one knew.
The audience laughs, then stares in doubt,
With questions swirling all about.

A riddle wrapped in comic guise,
With jesters' fables under the skies.
Each chuckle leaves them wanting more,
While punchlines dance just out the door.

So revel in the joy we share,
In this grand show of wild despair.
For in the laughter's sweet embrace,
We find the truth in the empty space.

## Laughter Woven in a Tapestry of Questions.

A question asked, a punchline lost,
Like surfing waves, what's the cost?
We weave our thoughts in threads of fun,
While missing answers on the run.

Each giggle hides a deeper thought,
In silly stories, truth is caught.
The tapestry unfolds bizarre,
With threads that stretch both near and far.

Amidst confusions, joy ignites,
In laughter's heart, we find delights.
The queries linger, answers stray,
But laughter leads us on the way.

So take a stroll on whimsy's path,
In playful moments, savor the laugh.
For though the punchline may elude,
The journey's worth, in merry mood.

## Existential Shenanigans

A clown with thoughts all out of place,
Wonders if he's missed the race.
He juggles dreams with vibrant glee,
In search of truths, yet blind to see.

On stage of life, a skit unfolds,
With tales of wisdom that rarely hold.
Each laugh erupts, a fleeting light,
Yet mystery shrouds the dead of night.

Amid the chaos, a question gleams,
What's real, what's part of our dreams?
In shenanigans that tip the scales,
We chase the punchline, but it fails.

So parenthesis the world we know,
With sideshow antics and wild show.
For amidst the jest and whimsical cheer,
The essence of absurdity draws near.

## The Riddle Without an Answer

A riddle sits with a crooked smile,
It teases minds to ponder a while.
What's the punchline? Oh, where did it go?
We laugh and scratch, yet don't really know.

The humorous twist gets tangled tight,
As we seek out the meaning in the night.
In loops of humor and thoughts entwined,
The punchline dances, forever blind.

A riddle rolls in a wheel of chance,
With jesters leaping in a silly dance.
We chase shadows of thoughts profound,
Searching for giggles that swirl around.

So here we stand, both lost and found,
In riddles echoed, with laughter bound.
For in this quest, the heart's delight,
Is losing track of the punchline's flight.

## Chasing Shadows of Jokes

In the park, we laugh and play,
Chasing shadows that run away.
Punchlines hide behind a tree,
Whispers giggle, 'Come find me!'

Puns float like clouds in the air,
Tickling thoughts beyond compare.
A slip on a banana peel,
Leaves us dizzy, oh what a reel!

Each jest a fleeting, bright parade,
Wit and whimsy serenade.
But the finale's lost the beat,
An echo fades, incomplete.

So we dance with every blunder,
Find the joy beneath the thunder.
A chuckle in the fading light,
Chasing shadows into the night.

## The Heartbeat of Absurdity

In a world where penguins fly,
Chickens race and dolphins sigh.
Time wobbles like a jelly bean,
Logic's taken a backseat scene.

Tickling under the big top hat,
Paragraphs dressed as a purring cat.
Every giggle a merry cheer,
Absurdity's heartbeat drawing near.

A circus act with no real aim,
Clowns with prowess but no fame.
They tumble, fumble, take a bow,
Left us pondering what and how.

So we laugh, though we don't quite know,
In a realm of whimsical flow.
Where bizarre is just a good friend,
And nonsense often comes to mend.

## Fables Without a Moral

A turtle raced with a hungry fox,
Riddles danced on an empty box.
The grasshopper played a tune so sweet,
While the ant just tapped his feet.

Stories twist like a ribbon spun,
No lesson learned, just silly fun.
A lion sneezed, the mice all cheered,
In this world, the strange is revered.

A cloud wore shoes, just to fit in,
While raindrops laughed at the day's whim.
Each page turned, no truths defined,
Just laughter tangled in the mind.

So let's gather round for a spin,
With fables woven thick with grin.
Where every tale's a jolly dance,
And morals? They're lost in the chance.

## **Whimsy on a Windy Day**

Kites chase clouds in the sunny sky,
While dandelions wave their goodbye.
A breeze that comes with a playful sigh,
Whispers secrets as it rushes by.

Birds wear hats and do the cha-cha,
You'd laugh too, if you saw the drama.
A tumbleweed rolls past the slide,
Together we laugh at the windy ride.

Each gust carries off our worries,
We dance to nature's light flurries.
The trees lean in, gossiping leaves,
They chuckle and joke, as the heart believes.

On this windy whimsy spree,
We find the joy, just you and me.
Where laughter swirls and troubles sway,
And nonsense reigns on a windy day.

## Searching for Laughter in the Dark

In shadows deep where giggles hide,
I seek a joke, a friend beside.
With every stumble, a whispered sigh,
Is laughter lurking? Oh me, oh my.

The moonlight plays a game with me,
A punchline lost, it's plain to see.
I trip on puns like scattered leaves,
Where humor flourishes, hope deceives.

Each corner turned, a grin will flare,
But then it vanishes, just thin air.
In this dark dance, an absence bright,
I laugh at shadows, lost in night.

How funny, this chase I undertake,
For giggles hiding make my heart ache.
Still, I wander 'neath the starry dome,
Searching for laughter, forever alone.

## The Unraveled Threads of Humor

In a tapestry woven with laughter's thread,
I tug at a joke, but it's often misled.
Each stitch comes undone, a whimsical tease,
Where punchlines fumble and puns just freeze.

The fabric of fun is worn at the seams,
As I chase the mirage of comic dreams.
A slip of the tongue, a stumble on cue,
Yet every mishap, a giggle to skew.

The more I unravel, the softer the jest,
With laughter elusive, not quite at rest.
A needle of humor, a threadbare delight,
Where jokes go to hide, out of mind, out of sight.

But nonetheless, I persist in my plight,
To gather the fragments, to snatch from the night.
For these humorous threads, though loose and askew,
Create a fine tapestry, with colors anew.

## **Chuckles Amidst the Chaos**

In a whirlwind of kids, dogs, and neat stacks,
Amidst all the madness, laughter attacks.
With every loud shout, and each toy that flies,
I chuckle at chaos, through tear-rimmed eyes.

The laundry's a mountain, a fable of sorts,
While socks have conspired, to flee from their ports.
Yet in the fray, a joke finds its way,
A tickle of humor brightens the day.

There's beauty in blunders, a slapstick surprise,
In tripping on toys, or slipping on pies.
With giggles erupting like popcorn on heat,
The mess is a canvas, still funny and sweet.

So hand me the chaos, the spills and the thrills,
For laughter, like magic, distills all the ills.
In a world turned upside down, it's my heart's little aim,
To chuckle through trials, and play through the game.

## The Lightness of Being Slightly Serious

In a moment of mirth, I find a sweet glee,
With seriousness poised, but not meant to be.
I wear my best smile with a twist and a frown,
For moments of nonsense bring joy to the town.

I ponder the riddles of humor so sleek,
With one eyebrow raised, and a curious peek.
If laughter's a dance, I'll step on some toes,
While frolicking through life, where the silliness flows.

With mischief afoot, and a wink at the storm,
I navigate pathways, with laughter as form.
Seriousness slips like a fish from the net,
In a world that's alive, and no signs of regret.

So here's to the moments, the giggles we share,
With lightness and jest, we lighten our care.
In the grand scheme of things, it's all a big play,
Where seriousness lingers, but laughter's the way.

## **Irony Wrapped in Smiles**

A tickle in the air, a jest on display,
We dance on the clouds, but the ground's on play.
With punchlines we chase, yet they slip and slide,
We laugh at the plot, where the truth likes to hide.

A clown with a frown, now that's quite the sight,
He juggles his woes, from morning till night.
Each chuckle a layer, absurdity's art,
We grin through the sorrow, it's all off the chart.

A riddle unsolved, like socks gone astray,
We chuckle and wonder, is this just a play?
The irony swirls, as we sip on our tea,
Finding joy in the chaos, however it be.

So gather your friends, bring the cookies and cheer,
We'll sip on our laughter, with doubts held near.
In the circus of moments, we dance and we spin,
Embracing the whimsy, through thick and through thin.

## The Giggle That Went Awry

A giggle slipped out, and then caught in a mess,
It tripped on a joke, and now it's a stress.
With laughter as fuel, we race to the brink,
Yet every punchline, is missing the link.

The toaster is humming with jokes of its own,
But bread never laughs, it just feels overthrown.
We tell tales of laughter, with marshmallows free,
And find every morsel just quotes from TV.

In shadows of humor, doubts quietly loom,
Where mile-long puns threaten to fill up the room.
A riddle or two, gone missing in space,
We giggle through air, yet can't find our place.

So let's raise a glass, but what shall we toast?
To laughter's odd journey, we love it the most!
In the chaos of comedy, absurd, oh so bright,
We search for our punchlines, embracing the night.

## **Laughter's Lost Thread**

A chuckle escapes, but it dances away,
It whispers a joke that was lost in delay.
With humor like bubbles that pop in mid-air,
We search for connections, but none are quite there.

We tickle with words that just fumble and fall,
Like kittens in yarn, we unravel it all.
The punchline is stranded, the setup unclear,
But giggles still surface, and that's worth a cheer!

Each pun is a tumble, each jest is a sway,
As laughter plays hide-and-seek in the fray.
With faces all smiling, yet jokes that won't bloom,
We gather the echoes inside the room.

So let's spin a yarn, though the thread's all a tease,
For laughter's a quilt, from moments like these.
In the fabric of folly, we stitch and we sew,
Finding joy in the quest, wherever we go.

## The Silliness of Being

In the circus of hours, we juggle our woes,
Balancing dreams while the silliness grows.
With noses like clowns and hats made of cheese,
We laugh at the simple, just aiming to please.

A banana peel slips, oh what a grand fall!
Yet somehow it teaches us to stand tall.
The riddles we seek, like shadows at dawn,
Remind us of laughter, even when it's gone.

While shadows of seriousness form in the light,
We twirl through the chaos, embracing the slight.
A punchline elusive, a wink in the air,
We chuckle together with snacks that we share.

So let's dance with the awkward, and giggle a tune,
For life is a jest beneath this bright moon.
With silliness wrapped in a warm, hearty meal,
We treasure the moments, together we feel.

## An Echoing Smile

In a room full of laughter, I trip on a shoe,
My joke lands like breadcrumbs, all scattered and few.
The punchline's a whisper, it hides in the air,
Yet everyone's giggling, not knowing I care.

The clock on the wall seems to giggle and sway,
Tick-tock like a mime, it jests every day.
I toss out a quip, like a fisherman's line,
It flops like a fish, but they laugh just fine.

A wink here, a nod there, the absurdities bloom,
Jokes float like balloons in an empty room.
I juggle my thoughts with invisible flair,
And they all join in laughter, though I'm just standing there.

So here's to the chuckles, the silly and sweet,
Each smile a reminder life's humor's a treat.
With echoes of joy in a world so divine,
We laugh at the nothing, a comfortable line.

## Musings of the Nonchalant

A cat in a bow tie just sauntered on by,
In a world full of puzzles, he's the wisest guy.
He yawns at the questions, rolls over and naps,
While I ponder the meaning of all the mishaps.

With coffee in hand, I sit and I stare,
At menus of choices that lead me nowhere.
The waiter just winks, like he knows something grand,
But I laugh at my hunger, it's all out of hand.

The wind whispers secrets of joy and of strife,
With every small giggle, it tickles my life.
So I chuckle along with the world's little quirks,
For laughter's the glue in this puzzle that lurks.

If nonsense were money, I'd be a rich fool,
In the game of existence, I'm bending the rule.
Each silly confusion a star in the night,
I'll dance with my musings, and hold on tight.

## The Enigmatic Grin

I met a wise owl perched high on a beam,
He told me my worries are all just a dream.
With feathers so fluffy and eyes full of jest,
He hoots, 'Life's but a riddle; forget all the rest!'

I pondered his words while sipping my tea,
Why stress over what's supposed to just be?
The muffins were laughing, the scones told a joke,
While I mulled over life with a half-hearted poke.

A jester's delight in the mundane we find,
With each little giggle, we shift our own mind.
So let's toast to the moments that swirl like a twirl,
In the dance of existence, let laughter unfurl.

Each curve of a smile is a riddle, a prize,
The secret of humor hides deep in our eyes.
So here's to the whimsy that life seems to send,
With an enigmatic grin around every bend.

## Smirking in Solitude

In the quiet of night, my thoughts take a stroll,
A tree waves a branch, like it knows it's on a roll.
The stars flash their questions, but I just moonwalk,
In the shadows of jest, it's a comical talk.

With socks mismatched and a hat on askew,
I ponder the wisdom in what I thought I knew.
The coffee still brewing, like it's got a bright plan,
And I sit with my thoughts, like a quiet old man.

The fridge hums a tune that's been sung before,
While I giggle at echoes that bounce off the floor.
In solitude's clutches, a smirk breaks the night,
As I dance with my dreams, oh what a delight!

So here's to the chuckles we find on our way,
To the humor of quiet in the light of the day.
For laughter is magic, even when it feels strange,
In the art of the solo, we learn how to change.

www.ingramcontent.com/pod-product-compliance
Lightning Source LLC
Chambersburg PA
CBHW051643160426
43209CB00004B/774